Alphabet

Neeru Vajpai

RED TURTLE
RUPA

I would like to give special thanks to my daughter, Shrishti, who has been my most important critic and the inspiration behind this book.
I would also like to thank the Rupa team, who provided valuable help at various stages.

This book belongs to:

....

....

A a

Ant

A is for ant
It has no ears. It hears
through its feet.

Apple

A is for apple
Both red and green.

Aeroplane

A is for aeroplane
It flies high in the sky.

Alligator

A is for alligator
It lives both on land and water.

B b

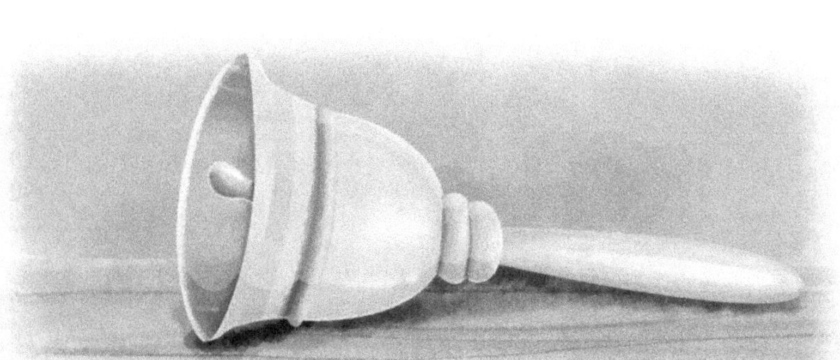

Bird

B is for bird
It has a beak
and no teeth.

Boat

B is for boat
It can go across a river.

Bell

B is for bell
That always jingles.

Balloon

B is for balloon
Light as air, it will burst if
you don't take care.

C c

Cat

C is for cat
Small and sweet,
it loves to sit under my seat.

Car

C is for car
It can take us far.

Clock

C is for clock
It tells us the time,
some can even chime.

Candle

C is for candle
It fills the room with
light when it is dark.

Dd

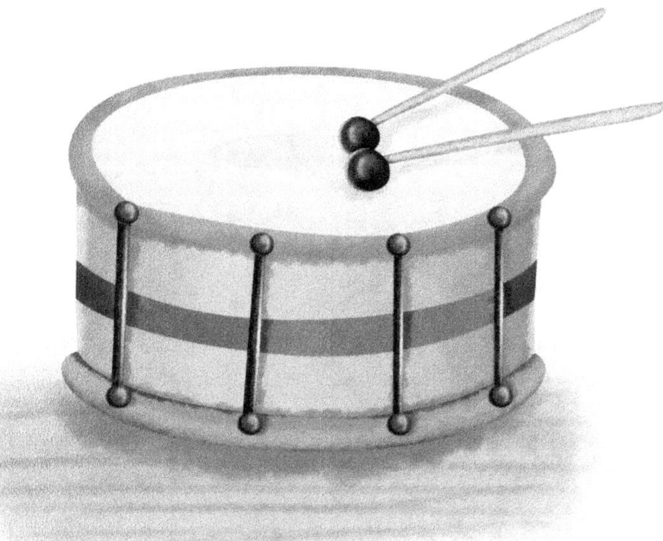

Drum

D is for drum
That I love to play
thump, thump, thump.

Dog

D is for dog
Mine is brown
and is always ready to
run up and down.

Duck

D is for duck
It swims in a pond.

Door

D is for door
To go in and out.

Ee

Ear

E is for ear
It helps me to hear.

Elephant

E is for elephant
It is huge, it loves to eat
leaves, shoots and fruits.

Engine

E is for engine
It pulls the train.

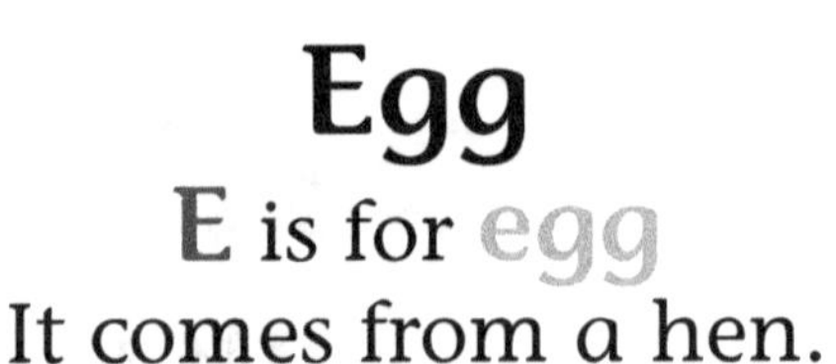

Egg

E is for egg
It comes from a hen.

Football

F is for football
That I kicked into the
net to score a goal.

Frog

F is for frog
Green and small
and the croak is its call.

Father

F is for father
He takes care of me.

Flower

F is for flower
It blooms in spring
when birds sweetly sing.

Goat

G is for goat
When hungry it bleats,
and eats green grass and leaves.

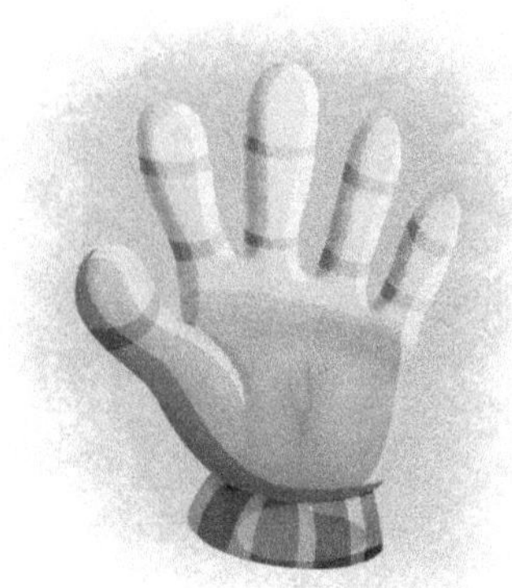

Gloves

G is for gloves
I wear them in the winter to keep my
fingers warm and snug.

Giraffe

G is for giraffe
It has a spotted coat
and a very long neck.

Gift

G is for gift
It makes everyone happy.

H h

Horse

H is for horse
It has very big eyes.

Hen

H is for hen
It lays eggs,
which are good for our health.

Honey

H is for honey
It is good for my tummy.

House

H is for house
Where I live with my family.

I i

Igloo

I is for igloo
It is a house of snow
built by an Eskimo.

Ink

I is for ink
It is filled in a pen.

Insect

I is for insect
They are so many,
some are harmless and
some are scary.

Ice cream

I is for ice cream
It is cold and sweet to eat.

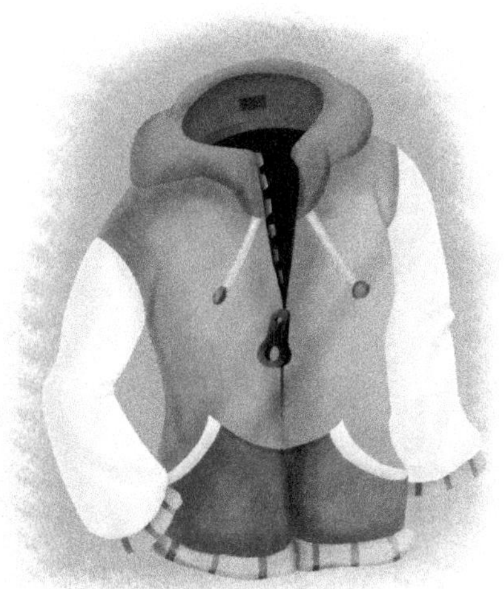

Jacket

J is for jacket
It keeps me warm in winter.

Jug

J is for jug
It holds a lot of water,
I can drink it all when the
weather is hot.

Jackal

J is for jackal
Its howl is loud.
It hunts small animals
and is very proud.

Jam

J is for jam
I love to eat it with bread.

13

K k

Kitten

K is for kitten
It loves playing with my mitten.

Kite

K is for kite
It can fly high in the sky.

Key

K is for key
It opens the lock
put on the gate of a
building block.

Ketchup

K is for ketchup
Made of tomatoes and yummy to
eat with fried potatoes.

Lion

L is for lion
It has a large mane that makes him
easily visible in the vast plain.

Lamp

L is for lamp
it gives me light
to study at night.

Lemon

L is for lemon
It grows on trees, yellow and round.
Once it is ripe, it falls to the ground.

Lollipop

L is for lollipop
Yummy and sweet, made of sugar,
it's a treat to eat.

Mm

Monkey

M is for monkey
They live on trees and jump around.

Mug

M is for mug
I drink milk in it
twice a day.

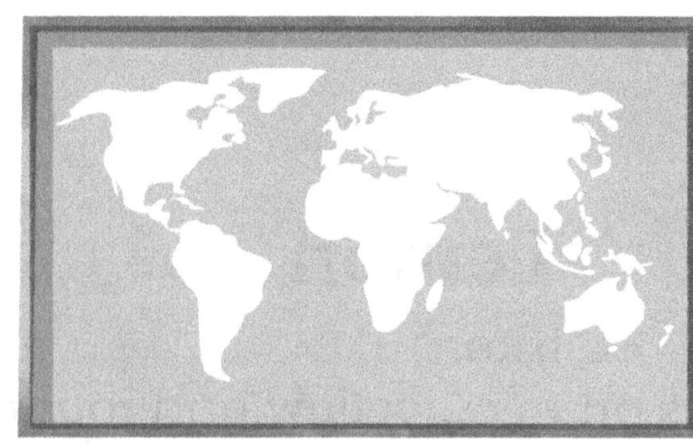

Map

M is for map
On it, the big round world
is shown flat.

Moon

M is for moon
It shines bright in the night sky.

N n

Nest

N is for nest
Birds build it the best.

Nail

N is for nail
Pink and small,
found on fingers of one and all.

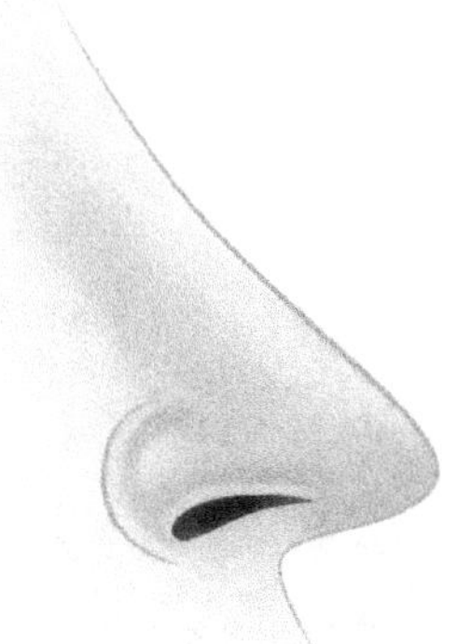

Nose

N is for nose
It froze in the cold,
when I went for a stroll.

Newspaper

N is for newspaper
Full of news and everyone's views.

Oo

Orange

O is for orange
Juicy and sweet, with many pieces,
it is easy to share and eat.

Owl

O is for owl
It sleeps during the day and wakes
up at night to fly and prey.

Oak

O is for oak
I sit under its shade to stay away
from the sun.

Ostrich

O is for ostrich
A large bird that lays big eggs.

P p

Peacock

P is for peacock
It dances in the rain
and eats insects, berries
and grains.

Pencil

P is for pencil
That we use to write,
it is made of wood and graphite.

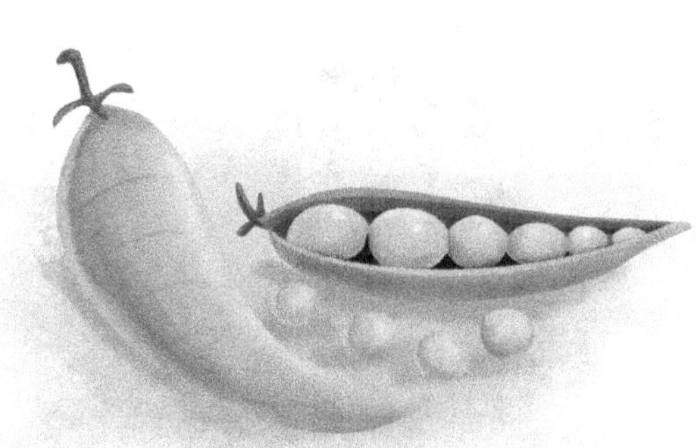

Peas

P is for peas
On a climber they grow
and stay together in a
small green pod.

Parrot

P is for parrot
It is green with a red beak.
It can repeat words that
we speak.

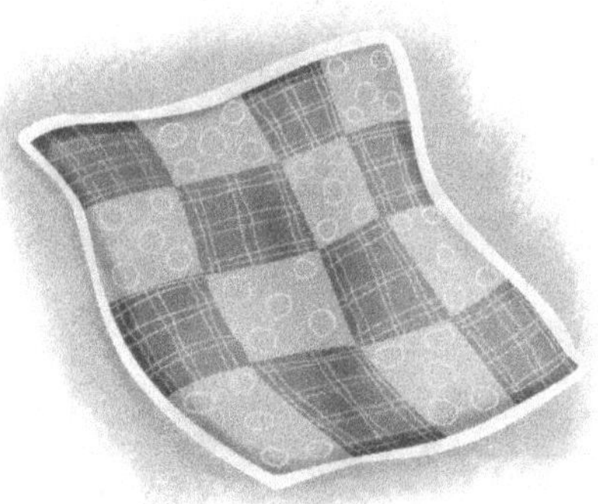

Quilt

Q is for quilt
Mine is red
and is spread on the bed.

Queen

Q is for queen
Powerful and strong,
she rules the kingdom and
punishes those who do wrong.

Queue

Q is for queue
And I have stood in a few.

Quail

Q is for quail
A bird plump and small, it is
sitting on a branch near the wall.

Rat

R is for rat
It is afraid of the cat.

Rose

R is for rose
Beautiful and red,
it has thorns that pricked me and I bled.

Rabbit

R is for rabbit
It loves to eat carrots.

Rocket

R is for rocket
It goes into space.
And it is so fast that no
one can give it a chase.

S s

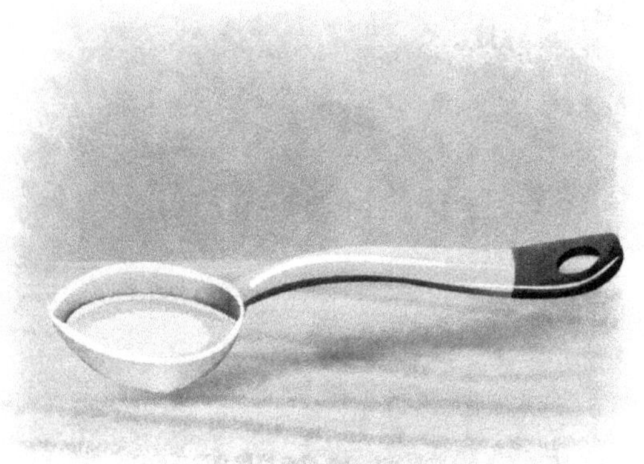

Spoon

S is for spoon
I use it to eat my food.

Sun

S is for sun
Big and bright,
without it we would have no
natural light.

Spider

S is for spider
It spins a web
step by step.

School

S is for school
Where I go everyday
to study and play.

T t

Train

T is for train
It looks like a caterpillar
on wheels.

Tree

T is for tree
With a brown trunk
and green leaves.

Tomato

T is for tomato
Juicy, round and red,
eat it cooked or raw, in a
sandwich made of bread.

Teapot

T is for teapot
Small and round,
it has a handle and a spout.

Umbrella

U is for umbrella
It protects me from the rain
and summer sun.

Uniform

U is for uniform
Mine is blue
and looks very new.

Unicycle

U is for unicycle
A cycle with one wheel
made of rubber and steel.

Unicorn

U is for unicorn
A mythical creature
with a single horn on its head.

Vulture

V is for vulture
It has a bald head
and eats the remains of the dead.

Van

V is for van
Used to carry goods, or to take a
family to picnic in the woods.

Vase

V is for vase
It is used to hold flowers.

Violin

V is for violin
It plays many tunes.

Watch

W is for watch
It is used to tell time.
I am always getting late as
I have lost mine.

Watermelon

W is for watermelon
It is green outside
and red inside.

Whale

W is for whale
It lives in the ocean
and swims using its tail
in an up and down motion.

Walrus

W is for walrus
The sea is its home and it
does not like to live alone.

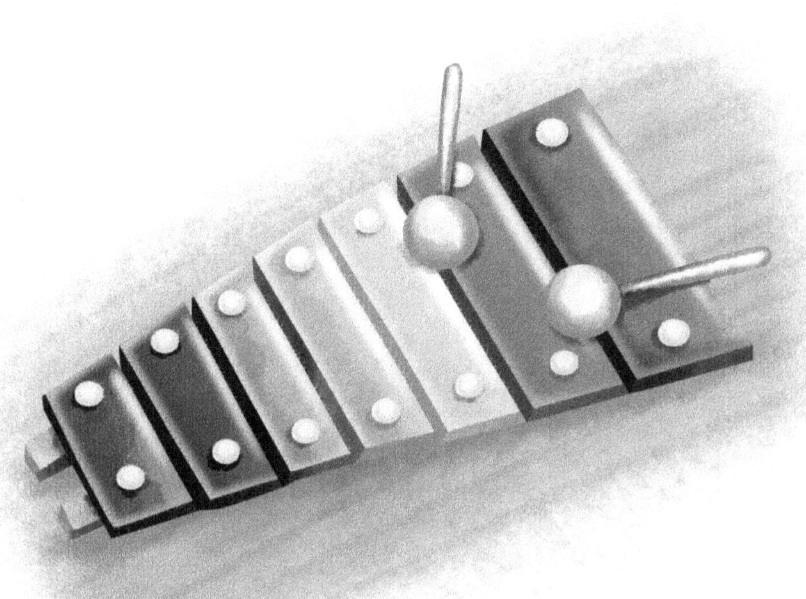

Xylophone

X is for xylophone
It can make music if you
play it well.

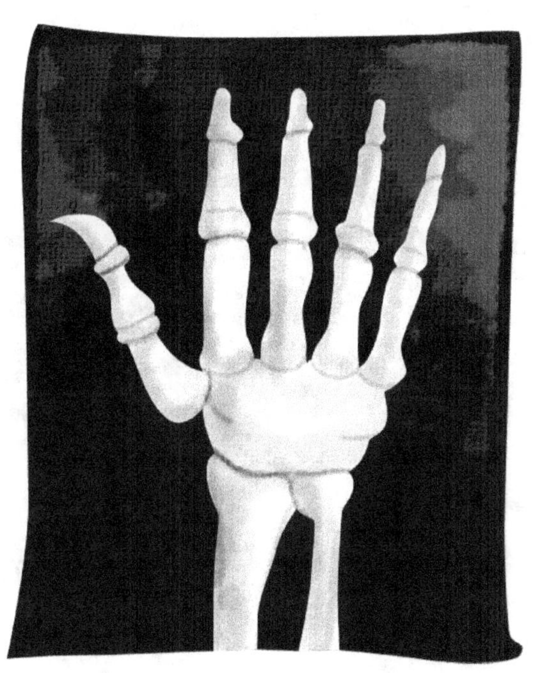

X-ray

X is for x-ray
It is black and white
and shows your bones
against the light.

27

Yak

Y is for yak
Black and hairy,
it looks very scary.

Yacht

Y is for yacht
That father bought
to sail in the sea.

Yogurt

Y is for yogurt
Made from milk and is white.
You can eat it in the morning,
evening or night.

Yo-yo

Y is for yo-yo
It is a toy
and playing with it
gives me joy.

Z z

Zero

Z is for zero
Its inventor was a
mathematical hero.

Zoo

Z is for zoo
It is the place where animals
are kept and birds too.

Zebra

Z is for zebra
It has stripes
on its body, black and white.

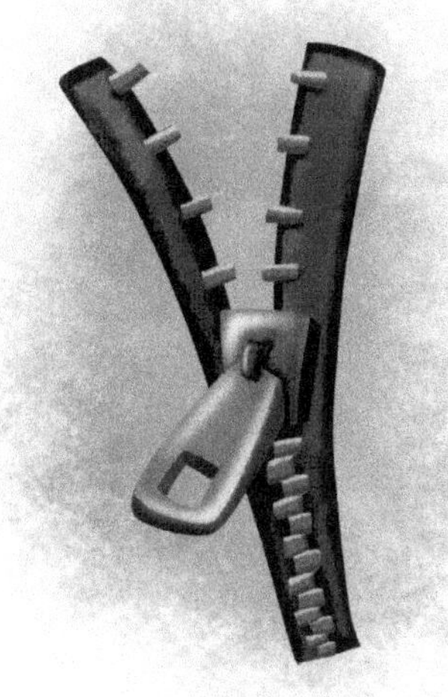

Zipper

Z is for zipper
On bags and clothes.

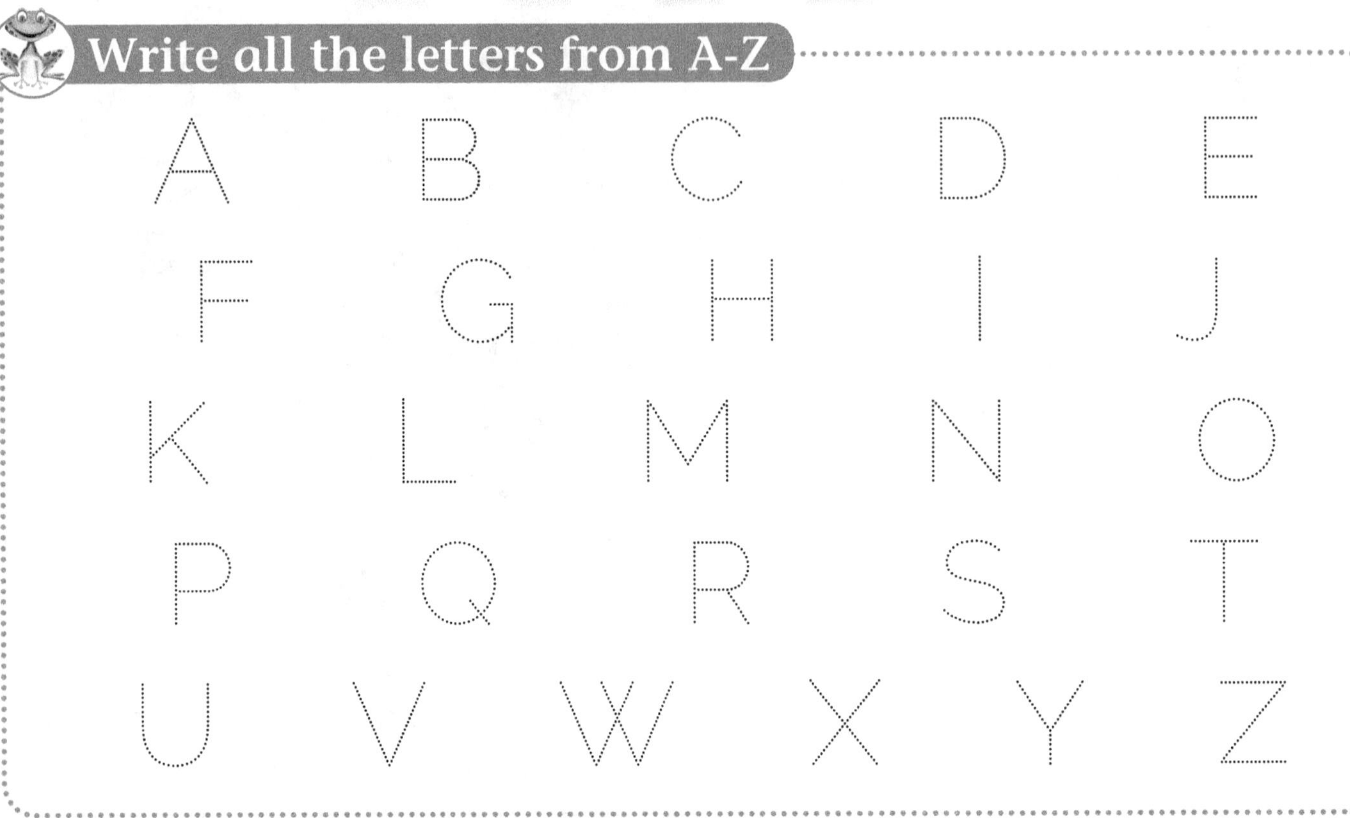

Write all the letters from A-Z

A B C D E
F G H I J
K L M N O
P Q R S T
U V W X Y Z

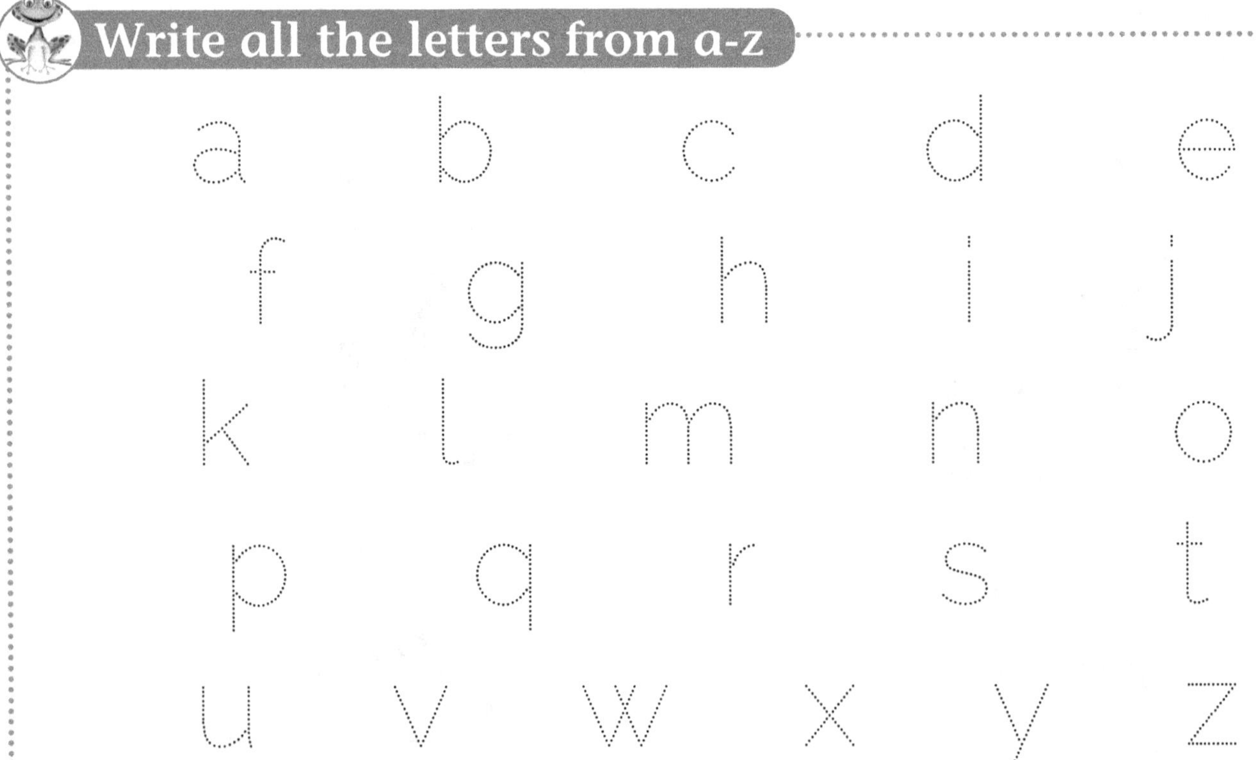

Write all the letters from a-z

a b c d e
f g h i j
k l m n o
p q r s t
u v w x y z

Write the missing letters in each row.

A B __ __

E __ G __

__ J __ L

M __ O __

Q __ __ T __

__ W __ Y __

31

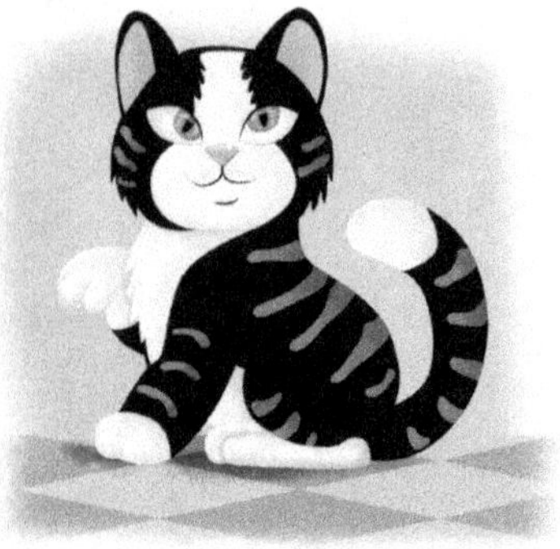

__at

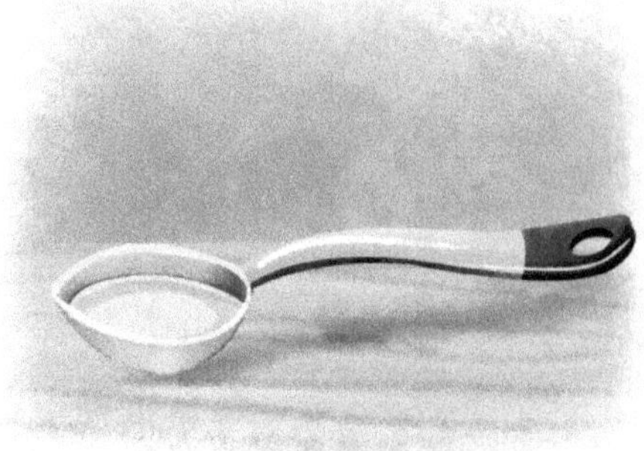

__poon

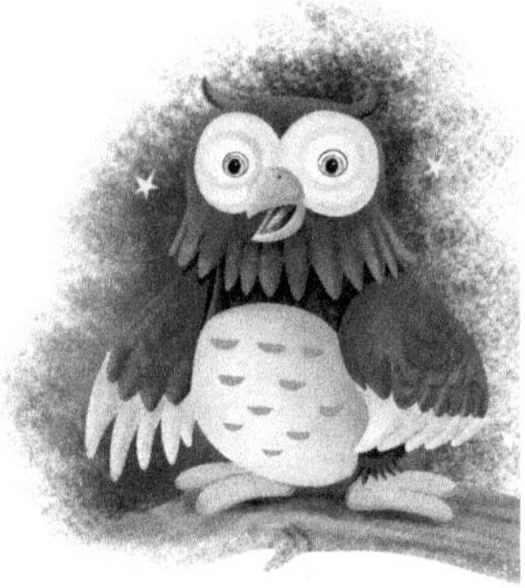

__wl

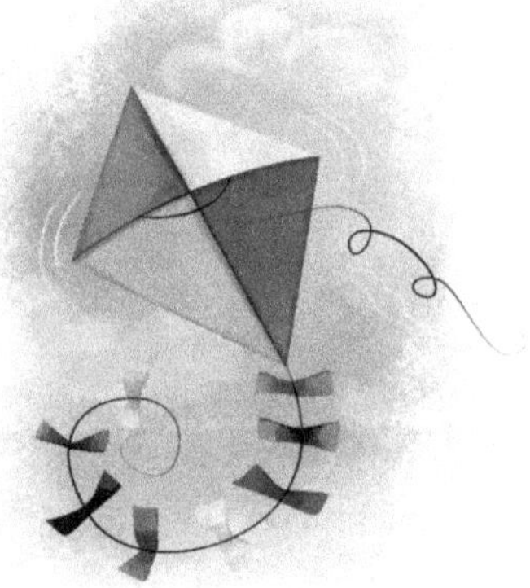

__ite

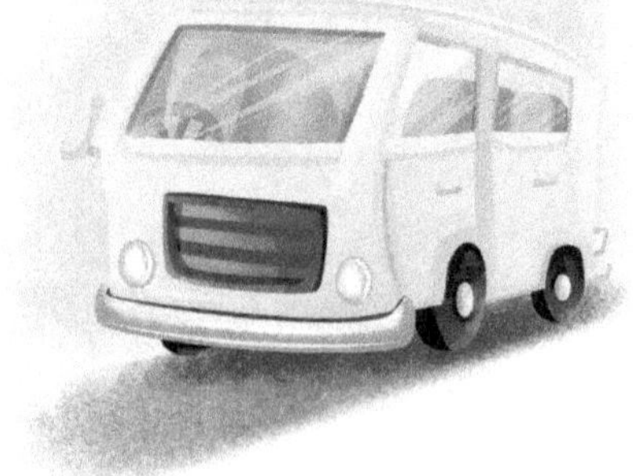

__an

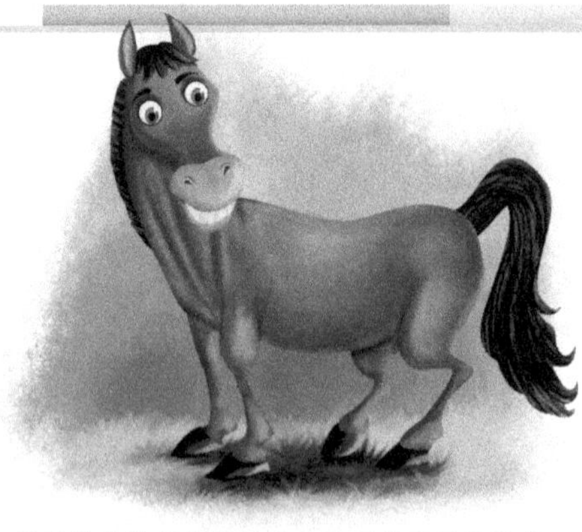

__orse